D0991747

Careers in
Explosives and
Arson Investigation

Fig. A

Daniel E. Harmon

rosen publishing's
rosen central

New York

Published in 2008 by The Rosen Publishing Group, Inc.
29 East 21st Street, New York, NY 10010

Library of Congress Cataloging-in-Publication Data

Harmon, Daniel E.
Careers in explosives and arson investigation / Daniel E. Harmon. — 1st ed.
    p. cm. — (Careers in forensics)
Includes bibliographical references and index.
ISBN-13: 978-1-4042-1346-3 (library binding)
1. Arson investigation—Vocational guidance. 2. Arson investigation. 3.
Arson. 4. Explosives. 5. Explosions. 6. Criminal investigation—Vocational
guidance. I. Title.
HV8079.A7H37 2008
363.25'964—dc22

                                                              2007035107

Manufactured in the United States of America

On the cover: A team effort: investigators at the scene of a fatal 2004 fire
in Kentucky include a state police arson specialist, a fire marshal, a utility
inspector, and a state trooper.

Contents

Crime scene investigation (CSI) has been a hot topic with Hollywood producers in recent years. Their television serials have generated a frenzy of interest in forensic science careers. Young people want to be like those CSI champions: men and women who triumph in scientific chess games against the cleverest criminals.

Fascinating careers in forensic investigation truly are available. They usually aren't nearly as glamorous as the small screen would lead you to believe. But they are rewarding indeed. The job involves, in many ways, a "scientific chess game" between defenders of the law and doers of evil. To expose and defeat the bad guys in real life, though, you may spend a lot more hours and days . . . and weeks . . . and months . . . than the television stars spend doing tiresome, thankless work. You will be frustrated, poring over tiny details that lead to dead ends. And after you've successfully reconstructed the details of a crime, you probably won't get to accompany the cops who have the satisfaction of arresting the criminal.

Some of television's fictitious CSI programs involve arson and deadly explosions. In real life, too, there is a need for

Actor Adam Rodriguez plays the role of crime lab detective Eric Delko in the popular TV series *CSI: Miami*. In this scene, he probes a suspicious stunt car fatality.

trained forensic arson and explosives investigators. These are professionals who can trace a criminally set fire or explosion from its smoldering destruction back to the exact spot of the first whiff of smoke.

What, exactly, is arson? The federal Uniform Crime Reporting (UCR) Program describes it as, "any willful or malicious [spiteful or harmful] burning or attempting to burn, with or without intent to defraud, a dwelling house, public building, motor vehicle or aircraft, personal property of another, etc."

A bored teenager's summertime "prank" of torching a remote, abandoned building is a fire-related crime. So is a money-strapped restaurant owner's decision to set fire to his kitchen, hoping to persuade insurers it was an accident. So is a terrorist group's plot to blow up a jetliner in midair.

Arson is believed to be the leading cause of nonresidential fires. The UCR Program relates that in 2005, 67,504 arson offenses were reported by almost 14,000 agencies in the United States. The average loss in property value was almost $15,000. One somewhat bright statistic from the UCR study is that there were 2.7 percent fewer reported arson offenses in 2005 than in 2004.

Arson investigators have two immediate objectives: (1) to determine exactly where, at the scene, the fire began and (2) what caused the fire to ignite. Explosives investigators need to know the same fundamental information as they probe the destruction of buildings, airplanes, and cars.

During their investigations, arson and explosives experts must always keep in mind a crucial possibility—that the fire or explosion may have been accidental. They examine fire marshal and manufacturer records that might suggest that the building or vehicle was at risk. They review emergency services and law enforcement reports that may document previous fires on the premises or similar explosions in similar circumstances. Their objective is not to prove a fiery disaster was a crime. They simply want to learn the truth.

Many different professionals take part in arson and explosion cases. They include crime scene investigators, laboratory scientists, and specialists in chemistry, electrical technology, explosives, mechanics, and other fields. Each is specially trained, and each has a unique role to play. They all take pride in their work. But they will tell you it is exactly that: real work. The glorified feats their fictitious counterparts accomplish on television are only a small part of what they do.

1

When Fire Becomes a Force of Evil

On April 19, 1995, American television networks were interrupted with a news alert. Pictured on the screen was a smoldering, multistory building with one side blown away. The Alfred P. Murrah Federal Building in Oklahoma City, Oklahoma, had been destroyed by a large time bomb planted inside a truck parked close by. Almost 170 people were killed, including many children in the facility's day care center.

Three men were arrested and convicted in connection with the crime. One, Timothy McVeigh, was eventually executed. He stated he bombed the government building in revenge for the tragedy at Waco, Texas, two years earlier. Federal law enforcement agents at Waco had confronted a heavily armed religious cult, resulting in almost eighty deaths. McVeigh expressed sympathy for the cult leader and outrage at the government.

How did McVeigh become a suspect in the Oklahoma City case? The bomb truck had been blown to smithereens. How could there be a possible connection?

It was a blackened axle fragment of the blown-up truck. Close examination revealed the vehicle identification

A truck bomb planted by antigovernment terrorists destroyed a federal building in Oklahoma City, Oklahoma, in 1995. Almost 170 people died; more than 500 were injured.

number. Agents traced it to a truck rental agency. Rental agency employees provided a police artist with sketches of the renters. Detectives showing the sketches door-to-door in the area found a motel owner who recognized the face of one renter— McVeigh.

In many cases, intentionally set fires and explosions are less devious, though no less deadly. Seton Hall, a historic university in South Orange, New Jersey, was the scene of one of America's most tragic dormitory fires. Before dawn on January 19, 2000, fire enveloped a third-floor student lounge in Boland Hall, a six-story dorm. Although the flames did not cause catastrophic damage, smoke filled the halls. Three students perished of smoke inhalation. Several dozen others were injured; some were severely burned.

Agents from the federal Bureau of Alcohol, Tobacco, Firearms and Explosives joined state and local investigators. Detectives soon suspected the fire was set deliberately, based on interviews with numerous students. They even had two likely student suspects. But they also needed to learn everything they could about the fire itself.

Specialists conducted experiments to determine how long it would take to ignite the suspected fire source—a banner made of construction paper. At a military base, members of the investigative team built a replica of Boland Hall. They made it as accurate as possible. They even installed couches made of the same material as those in the Boland Hall lounges. Setting fire to the model lounge, they videotaped their experiment, timing the progress of flames and smoke. Investigators repeated this process twice.

In January 2007, former roommates Joseph T. LePore and Sean Ryan were sentenced to prison terms of five years each in the case after plea bargaining. They said they had set fire to the paper banner in the lounge as a prank. It had spread to a sofa; the fire soon was out of control.

Who Are the Arsonists?

These cases were among the most sensational arson and explosives news stories of recent years. They suggest the broad range of fire-related crimes and motives.

Many arsonists are not really criminals. For example, a group of naughty children who strike a match to an unused, rotting shed at the edge of a field on a farm that belongs to one of their own families would not be considered criminals. Some arson events are not discovered until long after the fire has burned out, and some are never investigated. Officials are summoned to a scene only if an owner or observer sees that damage has occurred and cares enough to report it.

Disturbingly, some people who get kicks out of burning small, isolated structures begin looking for larger targets—targets that will make headlines. When they set upon massive structures such as an old mill, factory, or school building, they place the public at risk. Even if the building is abandoned, surrounding property may be affected. The owner may have intended to sell the building or to renovate it for new uses. Property worth tens or hundreds of thousands of dollars goes up in smoke. That is no small crime.

Arson becomes much more serious. What if someone is inside the building when the fire is ignited? What if that person becomes fatally trapped in a roaring inferno? If the arsonist is caught, a

A federal investigator looks on during cleanup operations in the aftermath of a paper warehouse fire. Officials suspected possible ecoterrorism in this 2004 inferno in Utah.

defense lawyer likely will argue that the death was basically accidental—the arsonist had no idea anyone was around. The fire setter, some believe, is guilty of destroying property but is not a cold-blooded killer. Still, in many states and legal districts, such a death is considered a class of murder.

In extreme cases, arsonists and bombers are indeed cold-blooded killers. Terrorists deliberately blow up automobiles, airplanes, and buildings. Malicious individuals set homes and factories aflame, knowing they are occupied. Killers in various circumstances set fire to crime scenes after the murder has been committed by other means. Why? They may hope the corpses of their victims will burn and vanish entirely, removing all evidence. At least, they believe, they can confuse investigators as to the actual cause of death.

Bizarrely, in some cases of property destruction, the arsonist is the owner of the property (or the owner's hired agent). Property ownership can be problematic. Homes and business structures frequently need major repairs. When repair costs seem too steep, an owner may decide total destruction is the best solution. If the owner's insurance company can be duped into believing the fire was an accident, the insurer may pay the owner a large sum.

Some schemers plot their own "deaths." A classic case was the Blazing Car Murder in England. In November 1930, a car was discovered afire on a rural road. Inside was a body, charred so badly it could not be recognized. Tracing the license plate number, police at first assumed the victim was the car's owner, Alfred Rouse. But Rouse was soon found alive. When questioned, he claimed he had picked up a hitchhiker, who'd caused the fire by lighting a cigarette inside the car. At trial, Rouse was convicted of murder by setting the fire himself. He wanted to lose his identity and start life afresh. Rouse was heavily in debt and behind in child-support obligations.

In an unusual serial case, ten members of underground environmental groups pleaded guilty to conspiracy and arson in setting fires to government and private property in Oregon and other states. The conspirators, operating for organizations known as the Earth Liberation Front and the Animal Liberation Front, targeted a lumber company, meat company, tree farm, police station, and other places between 1996 and 2001. Their objective, according to U.S. Department of Justice charges, was "to influence and affect the conduct of government, private business, and the civilian population through force, violence, sabotage, mass destruction, intimidation and coercion, and to retaliate against government and private businesses by similar means."

Sometimes arson is a hate crime. Churches and ethnic facilities have been targeted by religious and racial opponents.

Other arsonists don't care who their victims are, and their actions can't be explained easily. These are pyromaniacs, victims of a mental disorder involving a fascination with fire starting.

Damages and Tragedies

The damages caused by arson most frequently are material—partial or total destruction of property. During dry conditions, arson can set off raging forest fires that destroy thousands of acres of woodlands and threaten homes.

In the worst cases, arson results in death. Victims may die of burns, smoke inhalation, falling debris, or doomed attempts to escape. In desperation, they may leap from an upper-story window of a burning building.

All fires present dangers to firefighters and other emergency personnel who respond. Many emergency workers have been injured and killed at fire scenes. The most dramatic example is the September 11, 2001, terrorist attack on the World Trade Center towers in New York City. Many of the police officers, firefighters, and medical workers who entered the towers never made it out before the structures collapsed.

The Criminals' Tools

A single match can start a fire that destroys a huge, multistory building or a million acres of dry woodlands. Often, though, arsonists first apply gasoline or other flammable materials to the premises to make sure the fire will envelop the scene. Explosives, meanwhile, range from firecrackers to complex technological devices to vehicles packed with dynamite.

The most feared modern-day threats in this criminal area are car and airplane bombings. Terrorists sometimes use long-known forms of explosives. These include gunpowder, believed to have been invented a thousand years ago in China. Other explosives are dynamite and TNT (trinitrotoluene).

Terrorism has become a chillingly sophisticated danger. Criminals use newer, more subtle materials, including Semtex, a plastic explosive. Semtex is odorless, making it difficult to detect.

The flight deck of Pan Am Flight 103 lies in a field near Lockerbie, Scotland, in 1988. More than 250 people died in the midair explosion, attributed to a Libyan terrorist.

Terrorists who sabotaged a jet, Pan Am Flight 103, over Lockerbie, Scotland, in 1988 employed Semtex. When the London–New York flight exploded, more than 250 people died, including several on the ground who were hit by falling debris.

At Lockerbie, investigators were especially challenged. The aircraft had blown apart at a great altitude, so parts landed over a vast area. After gathering all the pieces they could find, they eventually were able to reconstruct the shell of the fragmented plane and analyze the source of the midair explosion. They determined that a radio cassette player stowed in the baggage compartment had been rigged with Semtex.

Most investigations of arson and explosions are not nearly as difficult. All, however, require tedious, methodical work by highly trained professionals.

Fiery Ingredients

Not all fires are the same, but all require three things:

1) Something to ignite them. This can be an explosive, the flame from a match, a spark, a candle, a burning cigarette, or a timing device. It can be a source of intensifying heat that eventually erupts into flame.
2) A fuel supply. The material being burned may be its own fuel. An arsonist might add flammable material to the fire. Gasoline and kerosene are common fuels that arsonists use. Many forms of paper, too, burn quite easily, as do certain woods. Some chemicals (those containing compounds of potassium and titanium, for example) are also highly flammable.
3) Air. Fire, like living creatures, needs oxygen to "breathe." Eliminate the air supply, and the fire dies.

Investigators are trained to read the clues. They try to determine how the fire was ignited and whether additional fuel was applied. How intensely and how long the fire burned can reveal much

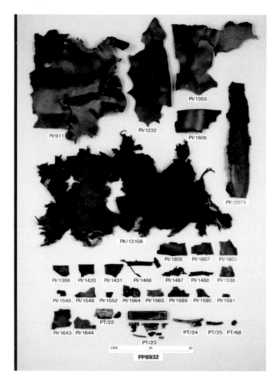

Fragments of a suitcase that contained an electronic bomb are labeled carefully. Forensic specialists determined this to be the source of the Pan Am Flight 103 explosion.

about the nature of the fire. If specific firefighting measures (water, chemical extinguishers) did little to control the inferno, that very fact can be a valuable sign for knowledgeable investigators.

Every explosion and arson scene is different and presents a new set of challenges to investigators. Meeting the challenges helps solve crimes. Forensic professionals render an invaluable service to society. A career in forensic science that focuses on arson and explosives cases can be especially rewarding.

Chapter

2

The Many Tasks of Forensic Fire Examiners

John Houde, author of *Crime Lab: A Guide for Non-scientists*, equates forensic investigation to the term "criminalist." He writes, "A criminalist is one who applies science to the law. This professional may be known by the name forensic chemist, forensic scientist or police chemist."

Different kinds of forensic examiners take part in explosives and arson investigations. Some gather all the potentially useful clues at a scene of fiery destruction. Others focus on single aspects of it: the state of charred human remains, traces of chemicals that may have ignited or contributed to the inferno, or details of structural damage that might suggest the intensity and duration of the fire.

Arriving at the Scene

Firefighters and emergency medical professionals are usually the first responders to fire alerts. Sometimes the causes of a fire are obvious. It may be a stove burner that a person admits turning to high before falling asleep on

Who Conducts the Investigation?

Forensic scientists who investigate arson and explosives crimes are usually employed by a city or county law enforcement agency. In certain cases, specialists from state and federal crime bureaus conduct the probe or assist local authorities. Federal entities that are frequently involved in arson and explosives investigations include the Bureau of Alcohol, Tobacco, Firearms and Explosives (ATF, an agency within the U.S. Department of Justice) and the Federal Bureau of Investigation (FBI).

Other forensic specialists on the scene may be insurance company staff or private investigators hired by property owners.

the living room couch. It could involve a smoker who acknowledges he probably dozed off in the bedroom with a lit cigarette dangling between his fingers.

Other circumstances are suspicious. Firefighters summon law enforcement officers, who may determine the situation calls for applied investigation. Forensic professionals are called in quickly. These experts might include general arson investigators as well as specialists—anthropologists, chemists, and odontologists.

A forensic investigator takes notes while examining the charred ruins of a South Carolina home in which a family perished in 2004. Authorities concluded that one of the parents had set the fire.

The job of a crime scene investigator (or "technician") is to examine a crime scene minutely and collect all forms of physical evidence. Items of possible importance in the investigation are placed in containers and given detailed labels. Labels record the time they were packaged, interesting characteristics, possible connections with other items, etc.

Careful notes are recorded. Sketches and diagrams are drawn. To help "preserve" the scene as it appeared in the aftermath, hundreds or thousands of photographs might be taken. High-quality videos may be useful.

Arson and explosives specialists look for traces of incendiary materials or devices. They study the scene of the fire to learn where it began and how it spread. Their thorough knowledge of fire types and causes enables them to re-create the event.

If a human corpse is discovered, it is taken to a morgue. There, a forensic pathologist will examine it and determine the exact cause of death. Was it smoke inhalation, trauma from the fire itself, or other forces—which might suggest murder? Pathologists know, for instance, that if no carbon monoxide is present in the lungs, it may indicate the victim was already dead (not inhaling) during the time of the fire.

Scouring the Ruins

The first objectives of the arson investigator are simple: to determine where the fire started, what caused it to ignite, and whether a flammable substance was applied to the scene to make the fire burn faster or hotter. But the investigation is often no simple matter. A special difficulty in arson investigation is that in many cases, fire-fighters unavoidably destroy much of the evidence while putting out the fires.

Fire investigators look for clues commonly found at other types of crime scenes: fingerprints, footprints, tire tracks, and signs of

Firefighters scrutinize ashes from a house fire. Minute examination can reveal clues that might indicate whether the fire began accidentally or intentionally.

breaking and entering. Meanwhile, they search specifically for indications about the fire itself. They carefully study the nature of the damage all around the scene. The pattern of smoke stains and charring on the outside of a burned building can tell them in which direction the flames progressed. The pattern of charring on thick wooden beams can indicate the intensity of the fire. The condition of door and window frames can be suggestive. If one edge is more badly burned than the other, for instance, it can show whether the opening was ajar or closed and which way the fire was spreading.

In seeking the cause of a fire, forensic specialists can detect traces of material that arsonists believed would be totally consumed in the blaze. A liquid or powder that makes a fire burn faster or more intensely is called an accelerant. Liquid accelerants include gasoline, fuel oil, lighter fluid, turpentine, and alcohol. Metal accelerants can include such combinations as aluminum and magnesium.

Arsonists, in a hurry or careless, often leave behind traces of the substance they used to start a fire—gasoline, kerosene, flammable cleaning liquids, or paints. Knowing this, investigators carefully gather samples of debris around the scene. A small quantity of a flammable liquid might settle between the boards of a wooden floor. There, it might be preserved from the fire for investigators to recover.

They place samples in bags or air-tight metal cans so that any telltale liquid chemicals that might be present cannot evaporate. Lab specialists will examine them for traces of flammable substances or explosive devices that might have been used.

Sometimes it isn't the evidence itself but the absence of evidence at a fire scene that makes investigators suspicious. In one case, a series of extremely intense fires left no traces of flammable substances. In the end, it was determined that the material used to start the fires was a mixture of metal substances that can create infernos as intense as that of a space rocket.

Law enforcement agencies often use dogs specially trained to detect fire accelerants. Labrador retrievers make some of the best "detectives" in arson investigations. Scratching and sniffing through the remains of a fire, they can point investigators to specific areas where evidence is likely to be found. These dogs' human partners are vital members of fire investigation teams.

The evidence-gathering stage of the investigation might take hours—or days, or even months, in extreme cases. Collected evidence is turned over to a crime laboratory. Hopefully, the results can help the investigative team determine exactly how the crime occurred and identify the perpetrator.

A canine "detective" helps probe the ruins of a fatal 2004 residential fire in North Philadelphia, Pennsylvania.

Inside the Lab

Laboratory professionals typically open sealed evidence containers under a hooded fan—a device somewhat like a stovetop fan installed in a home kitchen. The purpose of the fan is to draw away harmful fumes that might be contained with the evidence.

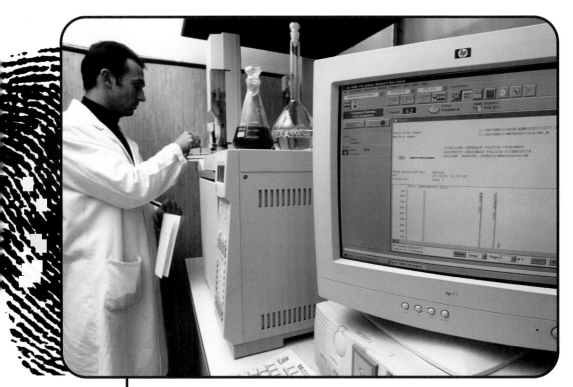

A forensic scientist uses a gas chromatograph to analyze a chemical sample. Gas chromatographs help arson investigators determine what material was used to ignite fires.

Forensic scientists use sophisticated equipment and methods to analyze evidence. First, though, they employ the ordinary senses of sight and scent. In many cases, suspicious substances on carpet or wood samples from a crime scene are plain to see or easy to smell.

One tool forensic examiners use is the gas chromatograph. This device can separate a substance into the different elements it contains. It can determine whether narcotics or alcohol exist in a blood sample. It can reveal a specific type of flammable liquid that may be present on an item from a fire scene. Gas chromatographs are astonishingly sensitive. They can separate faint traces of certain elements that are as tiny as a billionth of one gram.

Specialists can even detect invisible vapors, essences of a liquid substance that evaporate into the air. They do this by suspending above the item of evidence a small piece of special plastic that is coated with charcoal. The coated plastic can collect vaporized substances rising from the crime scene object.

Another forensic tool is the infrared spectrometer. By means of a color process, it analyzes the molecules that make up a substance and determines their ability to absorb heat energy. All known chemicals—thousands of them—have been charted for their infrared characteristics. Analysts compare the chemical traces found at arson and explosion scenes to those they have on record, looking for a match. In this way, they can identify exactly which flammable substances may have been present.

A third lab instrument is the infrared microscope, which enables investigators to magnify spectrometer findings.

Often during laboratory analysis, scientists conduct experiments on small samples of evidence. They then compare the results with previous findings. They might burn a piece of undamaged carpet from the crime scene, study the substances its burning produces, and compare those results with what they've learned about carpet samples burned at the scene. This can help prove, for example, whether a flammable substance was applied at the crime scene to increase the fire damage.

More Drudgery Than Excitement

You might think, from watching crime scene investigation programs on television, that the job is one of constant intrigue. In reality, crime scene investigators spend hours on their knees, probing for possible clues and knowing their efforts may lead nowhere. They must go wherever the potential crime occurred, as quickly as possible. If it's in a remote forest during a winter ice storm in 10-degree temperature, or on a slippery lakeshore in a driving rain . . . that's the breaks.

There's one other drawback: although CSI teams in major cities operate in shifts, forensic specialists in most jurisdictions are few. That means they're always on call— days, nights, and weekends.

Will the Findings Hold Up in Court?

One final task arson and explosives investigators may be called on to perform is to testify in court. Lawyers on both sides of criminal cases and damage suits look for expert witnesses to support their claims. Fire investigators are among the expert witnesses in demand. Obviously, they need an understanding of the law and a familiarity with court procedures.

Because they know their work is crucial in establishing the facts of a case, lab scientists are careful not to be misled by the results of their probes. For instance, in analyzing a paint sample from a fire scene, a lab specialist may find there are two or more layers of paint, confusing in their characteristics. Sometimes questions remain, even after exhaustive lab scrutiny. The truthful answer may be the simplest: "I don't know." Fire investigators realize a piece of suspicious evidence might not actually prove an accelerant was used for starting or intensifying a fire. Drops of gasoline or oil on a suspect's clothes, for example, may have gotten there innocently—while pumping gas or adding oil to a lawn mower, for example.

The role of forensic scientists as courtroom witnesses is neither to make nor to break a case, but to explain objectively and clearly what they have discovered.

Chapter 3

Special Preparation for a Special Career

Experienced firefighters and police officers provide heroic service and know their jobs thoroughly. Without special training, though, they are not qualified to participate in a forensic examination of a fire or explosion.

A high school diploma is sufficient to launch a career in law enforcement and emergency services. Some level of advanced education, however, is necessary for forensic investigators. An agency may require that the applicant have an associate's or bachelor's degree in criminal science or a related study area. At a minimum, a certain number of academic credits are necessary. Either before or after hiring, the agency may require that the new employee obtain certified forensic training. If you are accepted, some agencies may enroll you for training at their own expense.

Often, job openings for criminalists specializing in arson and explosives require that applicants have diverse qualifications. They must be able to demonstrate competency in more than just fire investigation. Useful related areas of education and experience may include lab chemistry, firearms identification, technical photography, human fiber analysis, and general fire or crime scene investigation.

Agencies do not overlook the importance of basic firefighting experience. They usually require that forensic specialists first undergo standard firefighter training and actually work as fire-fighters. Many forensic scientists are veteran paramedics or police dog handlers, as well as firefighters and police officers.

A middle school student handles a human bone in science class.

Are You an Avid Science Student?

Your personal interests and strong subjects in school can indicate whether a career in criminal fire investigation is for you. A solid knowledge of chemistry will be essential to a forensic specialist examining evidence from fires and explosions. Biology is also important, especially in cases where fatalities occur. If you have little interest in science, you need to reconsider your career goals.

Specialists are busy inside the FBI's highly advanced forensics and evidence laboratory in Quantico, Virginia. The FBI assists state and local law enforcement agencies in forensic investigations.

An exploration on the Internet can give you a good idea of the special types of people law enforcement agencies need in their forensic departments. The Federal Bureau of Investigation (FBI) employs forensic professionals in its world-renowned Laboratory Division. It provides lab services to state and local law enforcement agencies and helps train the forensic specialists who, in turn, work for those agencies. The FBI provides on-the-job training for its own professionals (at least eighteen months for most lab positions).

But it looks for job applicants who already possess experience and education. The FBI's Laboratory Division advises online (http://fbijobs.gov): "Depending on the particular field of interest, the most useful educational background is forensic science, in particular biology and chemistry."

Lab scientists' chemical knowledge, both basic and obscure, has solved countless crimes. In a California case, it was found that a nurse had been employed at four different retirement homes at the times they were destroyed by fire, over a period of eighteen months. Initially, investigators believed all four fires were accidents, probably caused by careless smokers. However, when they learned the connection between the nurse and the four fire scenes, they searched her home.

One of the searchers, a lab specialist, was intrigued by a curious finding: two small boxes containing an odd assortment of items. Inside each box were common pain reliever capsules, a sharp pin, purple crystals, and a glycerin bottle. By themselves, each item was ordinary and unsuspicious. But remembering a high school chemistry class, the investigator experimented and made an astonishing discovery. He was able to demonstrate in court that an incendiary capsule could be made with the glycerin and crystals. The capsule itself looked harmless on the outside—like one of hundreds of medications aging people take regularly. When a pin was pushed into it, however, the glycerin and crystals, after a delayed reaction, combined to create an intense flame of "white heat."

Begin Preparing Now for a Career in Forensics

If you're serious about a career in solving fire-related crimes as a forensic investigator, there are steps you can take now to better position yourself for a job, when the time comes.

Learn all you can about the profession—not from television, but from police and firefighting professionals in your town or city. Get to know them. Ask them questions. Ask for advice on how you should prepare yourself for future entry into the field.

Explore the Internet for details and resources on crime scene investigation careers involving arson and explosives. Again, avoid the sensational sites; look particularly for government and academic resources.

Apply yourself more diligently to your science classes.

Take an interest in photography. The advent of digital photography makes it fast and easy (and cheaper than film photography) to process and compare images on a computer screen. Become an experimenter with a digital camera and image processing software.

High school and college students sometimes can obtain internships as CSI assistants. You may also be able to volunteer at your local fire or police department. Learn what prospects might be available in your area.

The nurse had punctured and placed these incendiary capsules in ordinary places at the retirement homes. Within minutes, intense fires suddenly erupted. She was convicted of murder in the deaths of sixty victims.

Education Never Ends

The best forensic investigators, or criminalists, constantly educate themselves by learning details about all sorts of subjects, ordinary and extraordinary. Forensic professionals specializing in arson need to know almost everything about different types of fire. They need to understand what makes a fire burn hotter at one place on a carpet than it does a few inches away. They must know the properties of various chemicals that cause a flame to intensify or die.

One way they learn is by experimenting with fires on condemned houses and other buildings. They study the results produced on various types of property using different flammables. They observe how long it takes for certain areas of a building to become engulfed. They carefully study the appearance of burned items after the fire is out and look for the kinds of material that might contain traces of flammable elements.

Knowledge of odd subjects can play a key role in solving crimes. For example, a study of the workings of clocks and various electronic devices can help an investigator decipher the fragments of an exploded time bomb.

An arson specialist *(far right)* and arson investigation students study burning patterns at Centenary College in Hackettstown, New Jersey. Centenary is one of many colleges offering CSI courses.

An extensive background in firearms and explosives is obviously useful. Education and experience in photography and photo enhancement may be a plus, depending on a specific job opening. The digital era has heightened the usefulness of cameras in crime scene investigations. In a 2003 case, investigators noticed faint signs of what appeared to be a shoeprint on a slab of wood. With a computerized imaging program, a lab technician adjusted the contrast and other aspects of the shoeprint photographs.

Photographers and Videographers

Professional photographers and videographers are increasingly summoned to join investigative teams at fire and explosion sites. They're wanted not just for their ability to record clear, close-up images of physical evidence but also to photograph bystanders.

Detectives know that criminals often linger around crime scenes, or return to them, out of a strange, morbid curiosity about the aftermath. Arsonists and bombers are believed by some to be prime "loiterers." It's been reported that some have brought refreshments to emergency responders and have even helped extinguish the fire and rescue victims.

She was able to bring out an identifiable pattern of tread, which helped verify that a certain suspect had possibly been at the scene.

Police officers who wish to join a crime scene investigation team first need a solid background in police routines. Generally, they must have worked one to three years at standard police duties. Foremost, they need to understand the proper handling of physical evidence at crime scenes.

Important Personality Traits

Besides academic credentials and a keen interest in the study of life around them, forensic investigators must possess certain personal characteristics. For instance, do you have an eye for detail or do you sometimes overlook the obvious? Can you find what's concealed? Are you curious as to how ordinary objects may prove important even though they seem trivial?

Are you a good team player? It's one of the first requirements of a forensic specialist, who must cooperate with other criminal investigators with different roles to perform. At the same time, you must be able to perform on your own. If you require constant supervision—someone to look over your shoulder and advise you at every step—you will be of little use to the team.

Another essential is a good set of communication skills. Do you hate the thought of compiling notes and writing detailed reports? If you do, you probably should look into another career because you'll be doing a lot of that as an arson or explosives sleuth.

Finally, you must expect to be frustrated. In countless cases, investigators are confident they've discovered the identity of an arsonist or bomber, but they know they lack evidence that will convict the individual at trial. When an insurance company pays a claim even though a fire was an obvious fraud, investigators must live with it and not be discouraged. They must be ready to apply their best efforts to the next investigation.

Chapter

Forensic Careers in Arson and Explosives Investigation

The glamorized crime scene investigation teams depicted by Hollywood are based on those in major cities such as New York and Miami. Even if you're highly trained, you may find it very difficult to land a job as a member of a "star" unit. Forensic investigator openings in federal agencies likewise are limited.

Most forensic specialists work for small city, county, or state police agencies. For many of these professionals, forensic investigation involves only a fraction of their work time. They function primarily as ordinary law enforcement officers.

Specialized Forensic Investigators

Successful arson and explosion investigations are usually completed through the efforts of specialists in various fields. Here are some examples.

Trace evidence examiners are lab scientists who analyze physical evidence after it has been collected

A lab technician wears sterile clothing while resealing a crime scene evidence sample.

from crime scenes. Their work is vital in many categories of criminal investigation, including arson and explosives. Trace evidence specialists typically hold chemistry degrees because chemical analysis of human remains and fragments of burnt property often yield key clues for law enforcement investigators. The tiniest specimens of blood, hair, clothing, paint chips, or glass might become the greatest break in solving a crime.

Because they are lab workers, trace evidence examiners generally work normal five-day weeks. They may be on call at all hours by law enforcement agencies, however. Trace evidence analysts need a college degree in chemistry or another accepted science. They usually have to be certified by the American Board of Criminalistics or by the state organization that oversees their field.

Forensic chemists work in crime labs to analyze physical evidence using their in-depth knowledge of chemical properties and reactions. The remains from fire and explosion scenes might reveal much more to a trained chemist than, for example, to a trained electrician.

Among their countless services, chemists can help identify the specific element used to start a fire.

Most forensic chemists work for government agencies. Their routine hours and their educational and certification requirements are similar to those of trace evidence examiners. Chemistry, naturally, is the preferred college degree.

Forensic pathologists are doctors who help in many arson investigations. They perform autopsies on corpses whose causes of death are in question for any reason. Pathologists use various processes, from microscopic tissue examination to X-rays. They are expected to pronounce the exact cause of death and to accurately estimate the time of death. In most arson and explosion cases, they can tell whether the victim actually died at the scene during the event or was killed earlier.

To become a forensic pathologist, you will need to attend medical school and then train during a residency period (at least four years) at a hospital and medical examiner's practice. After completing your education, you will likely be employed by a medical examiner's office run by your county or state.

Some forensic scientists who hold advanced degrees accept teaching positions at colleges and universities. Dr. Henry C. Lee is one example. He teaches forensic science at the University of New Haven in Connecticut. Lee has written books on famous forensic cases and is much in demand by law enforcement agencies as a consultant and expert witness.

Other Sciences Used in Fire Scene Analysis

Anthropology is the study of human beings—including physical makeup and characteristics. Forensic anthropologists can determine the sex of a burned corpse, its height and weight, its approximate age, and even its race and ethnic details. They can tell how a fire has affected the victim's skeleton. They know, for example, that infernos cause bones to crack and warp. They know that bones can shrink in intense heat.

These scientists can also glean clues from the color of a victim's bones. Yellowish brown bones usually mean the heat of the fire was comparatively low. White-charred bones suggest prolonged, very high temperatures.

Odontology is the study of teeth. Many burned corpses are destroyed to the point that their fingerprints are lost. Teeth and bones, however, often survive the fire or explosion. Forensic odontologists study the remains of teeth. Sometimes they take X-rays or make casts of the dental remains. They compare them carefully with existing dental records in quest for a match.

The teeth of a burned corpse can reveal clues about the nature of the fire. Investigators must be extremely careful in handling them, for the heat may have rendered them very fragile. If they are charred or scorched, a careless touch can break them into fragments.

Some agencies hire forensic doctors and scientists as independent contractors or as consultants. In others, they serve as law enforcement agents. That is the case at South Carolina's State Law Enforcement Division (SLED). SLED chief Robert Stewart explains, "They go through all the training a regular agent does, and we even utilize them from time to time in the field. It gives them a greater appreciation of what the agents and the police officers are doing."

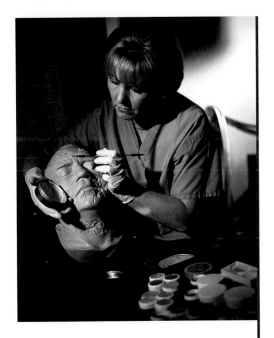

A forensic pathologist creates a model of a human head based on the corpse's remains.

Private Investigative Specialists

Aside from law enforcement agencies, who hires arson investigators?

Private employers include companies, insurance agencies, law firms, and individuals who have suffered property loss by fire. The manpower and other resources of police agencies can extend only so far. In many cases, when no solution is reached and no new

Related Careers

Careers related to arson and explosives investigation require similar types of study and experience. A bomb technician, for instance, is a professional called in beforehand to prevent a potential explosion or fire. In response to a bomb threat or the actual discovery of a suspicious-looking device, the technician's task is to disarm and dispose of the item. This individual, like forensic specialists in fires and explosions, needs a thorough understanding of incendiary materials as well as electronics and mechanics. The technician must know how all types of bombs—from crude pipe bombs to small, sophisticated mechanisms made with subtle plastics and chemicals—are constructed.

The FBI provides training for bomb technicians at its Hazardous Devices School. In county and city police departments, bomb technicians are usually volunteers who serve with the bomb squad as needed. Thankfully, bomb squads in typical police departments are required only sporadically. That means squad members spend most of their time as regular patrol or investigative officers, or as office administrators.

clues are expected in the foreseeable future after a lengthy investigation, law enforcement agencies must focus their attention on other pressing matters. Victims of these unsolved arsons, meanwhile, are eager to pursue the investigations. They may be willing to finance further probes by private arson and explosives specialists.

Although private forensic experts work independently, they do not compete with government agencies. Rather, they seek to combine their accumulated knowledge about the event. They compare notes and observations with police and fire departments. In fact, much of their primary information comes from the statements of firefighters, police officers, and other emergency workers who were on the scene.

Like agency investigators, private specialists compile careful records, diagrams, and photographs of the scene. Ultimately, if they can help bring a case to court, they must be able to back up their findings with solid evidence.

Many arson and explosives investigators who set out to work on their own have prior experience as firefighters or law enforcement investigators. Besides college and agency training, they are intimately familiar with fire scenarios of various types. They understand the "chemistry" of fires. They continue to take classes and constantly seek resources that will keep them better informed.

They also have to know how to run a business if they intend to earn a living. For them, college courses in business management are

A private investigator takes pictures at a 2007 crime scene in Elizabeth Township, Pennsylvania. Photography is one of many specialty skills employed in crime scene investigation.

almost as important as scientific studies. Many people interested in careers in forensic arson investigation have little interest in, or talent for, business administration. They want to focus on the science of crime solving. In that case, they must be able to afford support staff to handle administrative and clerical matters for them.

Be advised that if you're thinking of a career as a private investigator—in criminal fires or any other field of detection—you may face tough competition, depending on where you live and work. Besides former firefighters and agency detectives, many military police retire early and establish second careers as private investigators.

Some veteran arson and explosives investigators accept private work as consultants. They don't operate or work for private investigation agencies, but they agree to assist in investigations for industries, insurance companies, or law firms. These specialists include chemists, crime scene technicians, trace evidence analysts, and forensic pathologists.

Chapter

5

An Open Career Field

olleges, universities, and technical schools are establishing programs in forensic science and related studies. This trend partly results from advances in science, which have given investigators a new edge in the fight against crime. Another reason for the trend is the popularity of crime scene investigation serials on television. *CSI: Crime Scene Investigation* quickly became popular after it first aired on CBS in 2000. Two newer series, *CSI: Miami* and *CSI: New York*, also became very popular.

The TV series—fascinating but not completely realistic—have had several effects on America's law enforcement and judicial systems. According to a May 2007 article in *New Yorker* magazine, judges and investigators observe that many jurors in court trials are influenced by the serials. Americans have come to expect that forensic experts equipped with the latest technology can link the crime by some microscopic clue to the guilty person. The roles of TV crime scene investigators and laboratory personnel are both intriguing and heroic. Not surprisingly, applications for forensic investigative jobs have increased.

Students in a criminal justice class in Virginia examine a simulated crime scene and record notes. The scenario included a body, gun replicas, and specimens of a bloodlike liquid.

Because of the growing potential of forensic science, there is an increased demand by law enforcement agencies for colleges to produce qualified specialists. At the same time, more and more young people have become interested in forensics as a career, and they are looking for colleges that provide specialty training.

Examples of College Programs

As of 2006, about twenty American universities offered bachelor of science degrees in forensic science. At least twenty other

A professor and students study a chemical solution in a forensic science class at Virginia Commonwealth University in Richmond, Virginia. Knowledge of the sciences is essential in forensic investigation.

institutions offered associate degrees, certificate programs, or specialized degrees within the field (for example, forensic odontology). Educational opportunities have been developed by online universities and by traditional institutions expanding their distance-learning curricula.

Here are several examples of college degree programs in forensic science and the types of classes you will be expected to complete.

Virginia Commonwealth University, Richmond, Virginia (http://www.vcu.edu).Virginia Commonwealth offers both bachelor's and master's degrees in forensic science. The bachelor's degree is structured to prepare students for "effective professional careers in forensic laboratories, public and private, basic research laboratories, clinical laboratories, and/or to pursue graduate studies." Among the course topics are introductory classes and labs in biological science; general, organic, and physical chemistry classes and labs; life science studies; physics and calculus classes; classes in crime scene search and recovery techniques and analysis; forensic microscopy studies; a class in forensic evidence, law, and criminal procedure; and more. VC's master's program trains graduate students for forensic careers in government and private labs. Master's candidates select a specialized track within the program: forensic biology, forensic chemistry/drugs and toxicology, forensic chemistry/trace, or forensic physical evidence. In addition to specialized classes for each track, each candidate must complete a dozen core classes, such as firearm and tool mark identification and forensic microscopy.

Columbia College of Missouri, Columbia, Missouri
  (http://www.ccis.edu). Columbia College of Missouri's bachelor's degree in forensic science prepares students for both field and laboratory careers. Beyond general criminal justice courses, students must complete multiple core classes in chemistry and biology as well as calculus and analytic geometry, physics, and criminalistics. They then choose advanced courses in chemistry or biology. Elective subjects range from anatomy and microbiology to crime scene photography and forensic anthropology.

San Jose State University, San Jose, California
(http://www.sjsu.edu). Two emphasis areas are available within
the university's bachelor of science forensic science degree
program: biology and chemistry. As you would expect, heavy
course loads and lab work are required in the respective focus
areas. In addition, all students in the program must take classes
in criminal law, criminal evidence and procedures, principles of
investigation, criminalistics, and writing.

Wichita State University, Wichita, Kansas
(http://www.wichita.edu). The bachelor of science in forensic
sciences program at Wichita State is intended to educate
"forensic generalists, rather than narrowly focused specialists."
The university advises, "Successful students in this program
should have a strong aptitude [capability] in the physical, biological,
and chemical sciences. An ability to understand criminal moti-
vation and apply broad criminological theory is also important."
The program includes various classes in chemistry, biology,
anthropology, psychology, criminal justice, and forensic science.
Forensic arson analysis is part of the latter topic.

Villa Julie College, Stevenson, Maryland
(http://apps.vjc.edu/courses/forensic-science.cfm). Villa Julie
College offers a sixteen-month master's degree program in
forensic science for interested undergraduates in chemistry,

A graduate student in forensic science studies blood stain and tool mark patterns. This is part of course work at the University of Central Oklahoma in Edmond, Oklahoma.

biology, or related sciences. The master's program is built around "highly specialized training in the sciences, a core of law courses, and culminates in a thesis based upon original research." It is conducted in conjunction with the Maryland State Police Forensic Sciences Division. The program includes classes in forensic science, microscopy, physical evidence and crime scene investigation, trace evidence, safety and quality control, DNA analysis, and other subjects.

Trent University, Peterborough, Oshawa, Ontario (http://www.trentu.ca). Among Canadian universities offering forensic science degrees is Trent University in Ontario. Trent's four-year program "integrates the study of science, law, and investigative practice and theory." It is conducted in cooperation with the Centre for Law and Justice at Fleming College. Pointing out that "the forensic scientist is first and foremost a scientist," the university tells prospective students to be committed to rigorous scientific methods. Lab and field techniques in anthropology, biology, and chemistry are emphasized. Besides science, students learn to work as team members. They also learn about legal issues involved in their work.

Look for colleges or technical schools that offer forensic science majors or study areas. You may be pleasantly surprised to find that institutions close to where you live have just what you want.

New Job Prospects

The future is promising for people interested in forensic careers in arson and explosives investigation. A leading reason for that, tragically, is the increase in those crimes in the growing population. Americans still read about the same kinds of arson cases that have plagued society for centuries. In addition, their world is shaken by twenty-first-century terrorist strikes.

Another, positive, reason for the bright job market is the advance in technology. Technology allows professionals to gather and scrutinize the tiniest particles of physical evidence collected from fire scenes. Other types of new equipment enable experts to analyze this evidence from angles and perspectives that were impossible until now.

Aspiring forensic investigators who master these developing technologies will have an advantage in their job quests. A wide variety of specific careers are available—and the job satisfaction is immense.

accelerant A substance that speeds up a process such as fire.

anatomy The detailed study of the human body and other organisms by dissecting their parts.

anthropology The study of human beings, including their physical makeup.

autopsy The dissection and examination of a corpse, mainly to determine the cause of death.

charred Partially burned.

curricula A program or course of study.

flammable Subject to fast or intense burning.

forensic Related to the application of science to law.

ignite To cause to burn.

incendiary Capable of starting a fire.

malicious Having a desire to cause pain, injury, or harm.

microbiology The study of microscopic life forms.

microscopy Investigation by means of a microscope.

morgue Place where corpses are kept until they are examined.

odontology The study of teeth.

pathologist One who studies diseases or deviations from normal healthy conditions of the body.

pyromaniac A person with an irresistible urge to set fires.

toxicology The science of poisons and their effects.

trace evidence A tiny amount of accelerant, blood, or another possible clue at a crime scene.

American Academy of Forensic Sciences

410 N. 21st Street

Colorado Springs, CO 80904

(719) 636-1100

Web site: http://www.aafs.org

A nonprofit professional society seeking "justice through the application of science to the processes of law." Its members include criminalists of various types. Check out the "Choosing a Career" page at http://www.aafs.org/default.asp?section_id=resources&page_id=choosing_a_career.

Bureau of Alcohol, Tobacco, Firearms and Explosives

650 Massachusetts Avenue, Room 8400

Washington, DC 20226

(202) 927-8480

Web site: http://www.atf.gov

The federal agency dedicated to enforcing federal criminal laws and regulating the explosives and firearms industries. See specifically the bureau's Web section on arson and explosives at http://www.atf.gov/explarson/index.htm.

Canadian Society of Forensic Science

P.O. Box 37040

3332 McCarthy Road

Ottawa, ON K1V 0W0

Canada

Web site: http://www.csfs.ca

A nonprofit professional organization seeking to "maintain professional standards, and to promote the study and enhance the stature of forensic science" in Canada. It includes a careers page with contact information for police and laboratory agencies and educational programs (http://ww2.csfs.ca/csfs_page.aspx?ID=25).

Federal Bureau of Investigation

J. Edgar Hoover Building

935 Pennsylvania Avenue NW

Washington, DC 20535-0001

Web site: http://www.fbi.gov

The principal investigative arm of the U.S. Department of Justice. Besides investigating specific crimes, it assists state and local law enforcement agencies. It provides, among other services, forensic laboratory examination.

Web Sites

Due to the changing nature of Internet links, Rosen Publishing has developed an online list of Web sites related to the subject of this book. This site is updated regularly. Please use this link to access the list:

http://www.rosenlinks.com/cif/exar

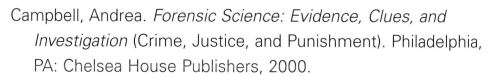

Campbell, Andrea. *Forensic Science: Evidence, Clues, and Investigation* (Crime, Justice, and Punishment). Philadelphia, PA: Chelsea House Publishers, 2000.

Ford, Jean. *Explosives and Arson Investigation* (Forensics: The Science of Crime-Solving). Philadelphia, PA: Mason Crest Publishers, 2005.

Fridell, Ron. *Forensic Science* (Cool Science). Minneapolis, MN: Lerner, 2007.

Harmon, Daniel E. *The FBI* (Crime, Justice, and Punishment). Philadelphia, PA: Chelsea House Publishers, 2001.

Murdico, Suzanne J. *Bomb Squad Experts* (Extreme Careers). New York, NY: Rosen Publishing Group, Inc., 2004.

Sapse, Danielle. *Legal Aspects of Forensics* (Inside Forensic Science). New York, NY: Chelsea House Publishers, 2006.

Shone, Rob. *Corpses and Skeletons: The Science of Forensic Anthropology* (Graphic Forensic Careers). Illustrated by Nick Spender. New York, NY: Rosen Publishing Group, Inc., 2008.

Stewart, Gail. *Crime Scene Investigations—Arson* (Crime Scene Investigations). Farmington Hills, MI: Lucent Books, 2006.

Bibliography

"Blood Could Lead to Suspect in Fire at Funeral Home." *Herald-Journal*, Spartanburg, SC, August 15, 2007.

Camenson, Blythe. *Opportunities in Forensic Science Careers.* Chicago, IL: VGM Career Books, 2001.

Echaore-McDavid, Susan. *Career Opportunities in Law Enforcement, Security, and Protective Services.* New York, NY: Checkmark Books, 2000.

Ferllini, Roxana. *Silent Witness: How Forensic Anthropology Is Used to Solve the World's Toughest Crimes.* Buffalo, NY: Firefly Books Inc., 2002.

Fisher, David. *Hard Evidence: How Detectives Inside the FBI's Sci-Crime Lab Have Helped Solve America's Toughest Crimes.* New York, NY: Simon & Schuster, 1995.

"Four Defendants Plead Guilty to Arson and Conspiracy Charges Associated with Earth Liberation Front and Animal Liberation Front." U.S. Department of Justice press release, November 9, 2006.

Genge, N. E. *The Forensic Casebook.* New York, NY: Ballantine Books, 2002.

Gerson, Allan, and Jerry Adler. *The Price of Terror.* New York, NY: HarperCollins, 2001.

Gold, Jeffrey. "2 Get 5 Years for Fatal Seton Hall Fire." Associated Press, January 26, 2007.

Harmon, Daniel E. "SLED: Backed by the State Law Enforcement Division, Even Small-Town Police Officers Are a Match for Miscreants." *Sandlapper Magazine*, Winter 2003–2004.

Houde, John. *Crime Lab: A Guide for Nonscientists*. Ventura, CA: Calico Press, 1999.

Lee, Dr. Henry C., and Jerry Labriola, MD. *Dr. Henry Lee's Forensic Files*. Amherst, NY: Prometheus Books, 2006.

McGraw, Seamus. "Seton Hall: The Worst Dormitory Fire in the U.S." The Crime Library. Retrieved August 21, 2007 (http://www.crimelibrary.com/notorious_murders/young/seton_hall/index.html).

Miller, Hugh. *What the Corpse Revealed: Murder and the Science of Forensic Detection*. New York, NY: St. Martin's Press, 1998.

Owen, David. *Hidden Evidence: Forty True Crimes and How Forensic Science Helped Solve Them*. Buffalo, NY: Firefly Books Inc., 2000.

Ramsland, Katherine. *The Science of Cold Case Files*. New York, NY: Berkley Boulevard Books, 2004.

Thomas, Andrew A. *Aviation Insecurity: The New Challenges of Air Travel*. New York, NY: Prometheus Books, 2003.

Toobin, Jeffrey. "The CSI Effect: The Truth About Forensic Science." *New Yorker*, May 7, 2007, pp. 30–35.

Index

A

accelerants, types of, 24
American Board of Criminalistics, 40
Animal Liberation Front, 14
anthropologists, forensic, 20, 42
arson
    dangers of, 11, 14–15
    defined, 5–6
    investigating, 6, 17–18, 21–27
    reasons for, 11–14
    statistics on, 6
    tools/materials used for, 15, 17, 24
arson and explosives investigators,
  forensic
    as contractors/consultants, 43, 47
    education/training needed, 30–31,
        33, 34, 35–37, 40, 41, 45–46
    as expert witnesses, 28–29
    job duties of, 5, 6, 19–29, 38
    job market for, 55
    personal characteristics needed, 38
    in private practice, 20, 43–47
    related careers, 44
    specialties in, 7, 19, 20, 39–47

B

Blazing Car Murder, 13
bomb technicians, 44
Bureau of Alcohol, Tobacco, Firearms,
  and Explosives, 10, 20

C

chemists, forensic, 20, 40–41, 47
college programs in forensic science,
    49–54
court, testifying in, 28–29
crime scene investigation, Hollywood
    and, 4, 28, 39, 48
crime scene investigator/technician,
    21–22, 47
criminalist, defined, 19
CSI: Crime Scene Investigation, 48

D

dogs, used for arson investigation,
    24–25

E

Earth Liberation Front, 14
expert witnesses, 28–29, 41
explosives/explosions, 15–17
    investigating, 6, 16–17, 18,
        21–22

F

Federal Bureau of Investigation, 20,
    32–33, 44
fires, studying nature of, 23, 35
forensic science, college programs in,
    49–54

About the Author

Daniel E. Harmon is a veteran magazine and newspaper editor and writer whose articles have appeared in many national and regional periodicals. His more than fifty educational books include works on the Federal Bureau of Investigation, the U.S. attorney general's office, and other government agencies. He lives in Spartanburg, South Carolina.

Photo Credits

Cover, pp. 1, 12, 16, 21, 25, 31, 32, 36, 40, 46, 49, 50, 53 © AP Images; p. 5 © CBS via Getty Images; p. 9 © AFP/Getty Images; p. 18 © Getty Images; p. 23 © Michael Donne/Photo Researchers, Inc.; p. 26 © Mauro Fermariello/Photo Researchers, Inc.; p. 43 © John McLean/Photo Researchers, Inc.

Designer: Les Kanturek; **Editor:** Kathy Kuhtz Campbell
Photo Researcher: Cindy Reiman